SANDSTONE MONASTERY

Anson Wright

Wijiji Publishing

Published by
Wijiji Publishing
6312 SW Capitol Highway
PMB 177
Portland, Oregon 97239

Special thanks to Silas Halloran-Steiner and Jenna Scott. Thanks also to Diane Caudillo, Steve Engel, Pam Smith, Brian Arnell, John Herman, Katherine Cobb, Lara Utman, Jan Waldman, Nancy Steeler, and G.B. Cornucopia. Ted Owen shepherded the overall production, and the project would not have happened without him. Monkdream first appeared in slightly different format in the *Willamette Week. For Silas*, *Prayer for Carrie Claire*, and *For My Grandfather*, first appeared in slightly different format in *Openings*, and in *Mothers and Fathers: Being Parents, Remembering Parents*, both publications of Out of the Ashes Press.

First Edition
Printed in the United States of America
Library of Congress Control Number: 2004094172
ISBN 0-9758531-0-4

For my son and my ever-growing extended family

Preface

Located in a remote section of northwest New Mexico, Chaco Canyon is the center of a prehistoric Indian culture shrouded in mystery and unanswered questions. Like a bee returning to its hive, I have ventured there every year since 1989, often twice a year. My arrangement of these poems is an attempt to be true to that world, a world to which I am so drawn. I ask forgiveness that I rely mainly on my own experience, my own sense of alignment with the cardinal directions and what that has come to mean for me. There is not always clarity or neatness as I walk at Chaco. The sun does not always have a distinct point on the horizon with which to mark its travel. And I will take poetic license in placing some of these poems in a way that is less than tidy, less than obvious. Some may feel that the cornmeal I am offering up is much too modern, much too intertwined with narrow feelings and perceptions. You can only offer the gifts you have been given; I ask forgiveness again.

There are miles of ancient roadways emanating from Chaco. Their purpose is still being debated among archeologists, but many think that travel was not their primary function. The roads may not have been ways to get to a destination, but rather, a mirror of the destination itself; inscriptions carved into the earth which both praised and revealed a sacred cosmology. When the Chacoans left their canyon in the 1200s, they ceremonially burned their roads as if to consecrate and destroy with one fire. My poetry attempts to serve that function; something consumed and yet held sacred.

West to the Home of the Kachinas

My Children, like Rain Falling

My children,
like rain falling
perhaps our lives, after all
are only water.

Perhaps the single tear
contains
the soft murmuring
of all truth.
Our souls
fall from the sky
only to mingle
and rise again,
and I wait quietly
in this bed,
trading my pain
for the vision
dancing
in a winter's storm.

If I could announce
the sudden squalls
blurring my sight,
the memories
of each passing sky,
each fleeting rainbow.
If I could find one word,
hear one sound,
float without effort
beyond gravity's salty atmosphere,
enter slowly the kingdom,
sit at your webbed feet,
my fixed stare
an endless lake.

My sorrow
forms the shoreline
where our worlds meet,
red heart stinging
the bitter aftermath
of birth's cry.
We are made human
only to feel the ocean
within us,
our quickened lives
a storm cloud's shadow
upon the sea.

For one short moment
I know the equity of being
and non-being.
I know we are neither tears
nor rain
but both rising
and falling,
neither breath
nor the desire to breathe
but the still wind
at waters' center.
For one short moment
I find sleep,
forgiven.

Six Years Later, Saying Goodbye

Memories of my mother's funeral:
the old man in black
slowly turning the wooden crank
hidden near her feet
lowering her body
deeper into the coffin,
my older sister
stopping the town undertaker,
once a high school classmate,
as he tried to pry
the gold wedding ring
off her left hand, telling my sister
I only thought you
would want this,
my teenage son
asking me if she was cold
to touch
as I placed his warm hand
against her fingers
and fought to bring
my own body
into her presence.

I put my cheek
against hers,
whispered softly
into her ear
that I wanted her
to be safe
in her journey
and that I loved her.
White blankets
were wrapped around her,

a single red rose
placed beside her,
satin petals
waiting hopelessly
for eternal night.

Six years later,
to the very day,
I feel the dark shape
of that rose
buried deep within me.
I breathe its blackness,
palpate the soft skin
near my sternum,
search for the brittle shape
lying silent
without fragrance,
its tiny petals
clenched tightly
into a small child's fist.
My own hand moves quickly
from my chest.
I rub my fingertips together.
They are warm and soft, unwilling
to massage any deeper,
preferring to stay at arm's length
from my heart.

Quaker Castings

I am a cast iron stove
air tight,
with nickel-plated handles
and a built-in
smoke chamber.

Father,
we were forged
together.
Our shapes unknown
to each other,
cold iron legs
holding our separate
weights,
forever supported
forever apart.

There is madness
in oak's density
bowing only
to patient gravity.
Consumed slowly,
with great tending,
the small fires
of our lives
cannot tell
of our warmth.

We are museum pieces,
solid and heavy,
sitting in distant parlors.
Children are told
do not touch them,

they cannot
be touched.
We cannot
be touched.
We must
not touch.

In Memory of my Grandfather,
Floyd S. Colwell,
Died November 26, 1962 at the County Home

Waiting for dawn
in Wyoming.
Looking for bloodlines,
heritage,
amid the red and orange
of a desert morning.
Cotton ball clouds,
high above telephone wires,
ride on the callused palms
of my grandfather's hands.

My grandfather was a pioneer,
a telegraph linesman,
like early explorers
in Wyoming,
a pioneer
waiting in boredom
for the snow to melt,
waiting for the dawn
and some contact,
some heat
of the sun.

He was a drunk,
sprawled on the sidewalk
near my father's law office,
hiding in the shadows
of the local bar,
his brown hat and overcoat
my only memory, old
faceless man

my father avoided
when paying
for the Sunday paper
at the local newsstand.

All four children
were told
he was dead.
We grew up
in our small town
believing a lie.
He was dead to us
until my older sister
learned of the deceit, begged
me to come with her.
Come see him
before he dies, she said.
Come see the man
they have hidden
seventeen years.

I did not go.
I did not move from the
grassy corners
of my backyard, long
wet grass giving me safety,
dizzying comfort,
as I ran and slid,
falling and hiding,
far from his world.
I did not hear
the iron key
turning in the lock.

I did not see the long hallway,
the old man
alone in a chair
by the window.
I did not hold
my sister's hand
as she tried to rouse him.
I did not look
into his eyes
as he rose slowly,
introducing my sister
to the surprised matron,
"Mrs. Diehl,
I want you to meet my granddaughter."

He asked first about
my grandmother, still comfortable in
our family home,
unaware of our discovery,
then about each of us by name.
My sister told him
she never knew
who he was
when she pushed him
away from the phone booth,
made fun of him
in her haste
to escape his presence.
He begged her
to take him back
to the bar,
begged until his voice rose
and he grabbed at her.

She ran,
never to see him again.

I shield my eyes
from the orange disk sun,
adjust the visor at each rise
in this lonely Wyoming road,
look into the mirror
at my murky blue eyes,
still filled with
last night's whiskey.
In my parents' fantasy,
my grandfather's water sac
was filled with whiskey.
He was born drunk to them,
to their world,
just born no good
they told me
when he was cold
in a distant grave.

Born a family deserter,
they left him on the corner
near my childhood Sunday school,
waiting for the snow to melt,
seventeen years.
Born to cradle me,
I believe this day
in Wyoming,
through unknown
gray-armed dreams,
seventeen years.
And now,
at dawn,

his hot whiskey'd breath
whispers of courage,
whispers of what we were
to each other,
whispers
of what we can never be,
whispers and I strain
to hear.

For Silas

Silas, the moon was full last night.
I saw silver hair
about you,
dark-limbed fetus
in a milky womb.

I saw the silver hair part,
your momma's stomach split open,
your small
round head
slowly emerge.

Silas, it is you and I
who are separate.
I bathe in your light.
I feel your embrace.
I look to your home
through black sky,
our distance.
I have left you,
you and your momma,
left a sky
I knew too often
by its darkness.

I am reaching for heaven's brightness.
You are three
and know
my search.
I ask forgiveness
for I do not
love you less.
I ask forgiveness

that I do not
love myself more.

Silas
my dancer,
your movements,
your stillness,
our smiles,
words flowing,
hands touching
my breasts
my chin
my face.

Silas
my teacher,
your energy,
your freeness,
our joy
in each other,
our pain
in separation,
our silver
streaming
radiance,
our love.

Prayer for Carrie Claire Into Space, Eternal

She dreamed
your eyes turned
from blue to brown.

She dreamed
and you lay quiet,
floating,
slow turning galaxies
about your feet,
eternity
beneath your smooth
eggshell eyes.

Outer space
to inner space.
Twilight void
to pink cavern.
Timeless
without sound,
to timeless
with pulsation,
the finite beat
of a human heart.

We would call you
Carrie Claire.
We would summon you
with our tears,
with the warmth
from my hand
resting inches
above you,
fragile comet

asleep
in the belly
of a woman.

Forgive us
faint light.
Forgive us
the door opening,
the machine sucking
your forty day form
from its warm bed.
We meant you no harm,
even as our intentions
robbed you
of your life,
marrying us forever
in that moment
of your fate.

Godspeed
faint light,
the smooth and silent passage
of a storm
before dawn.
Godspeed
faint light,
your journey
back into
the stars.

South to the Priestess

In the Art of Making Love

In the art of making love
the power lies
in not killing
each other,
in the openness
of warm chests
pressing against
weakened hearts,
in the giving up
of one stranger
for another,
in letting time pass
within the twilight
of not being.

Baptism

In the late afternoon sunlight
Mary of Nazareth is standing waist deep
in the shimmering water
of the mobile home
swimming pool,
wet Christ babies
cradled in her arms.
I cannot hear her
over the noisy idle
of my truck
as she shouts directions
about parking,
her children pointing
to different paths
toward the chain link gate.
The sun is sinking.
The suntanned mother is shivering.
I am told to hurry
before the dim light in the sky
vanishes completely.
I change my clothes quickly,
not worthy to glimpse
such a vision.

I am desperate
to slip into
the holy water
calm about her waist.
I am desperate to take communion
in the approaching twilight,
desperate to loosen the grip
of past and present,
to find clarity and forgiveness

in the cool chlorine baptism of
one unfettered moment.
One clear channel
to simplicity,
her watery hand
on my forehead,
full of lyricism and grace,
past and present evaporating,
a single drop of water
containing all my confessions,
into thin air
forever.

Cubism

How does one tell
of a cubist relationship?
The needs are always met,
skipping stones touching lightly
on dark green pools,
yet touching fully
before moving
obliquely on.
She is relaxed
in our jambalaya sex,
unafraid as her small fists
jab into my body,
comfortable with being naked
instead of nude,
constant in her wisdom,
unchanging in her love.
And even in the gray tedium
of ordinary passing time
I am comforted
by the flat-surfaced stones'
constant motion,
grounded in a space
free from clinging,
unhurried by despair.
My only enemy
my mind's halting
judgement,
preferring a frozen stream
with ice-locked boulders.
A still landscape,
familiar in its inertia,
breaking my faith,

undermining
the angular peace
crisscrossing
my heart.

Mirage

My heart is wrapped in gauze.
My heart is stored
in a silk cocoon,
white gauze pads
crudely fashioned
about it,
dried blood
grasping them
like adhesive tape,
small heart
suspended in a cavern
deep beneath the earth.

I sense its absence
in my chest,
place my hand
alongside my neck
to find its pulse.
The faintness
frightens me,
like instant coffee
made too thin,
like blood
no longer red.

My heart has left me,
hung itself
in another place.
I am living
and not alive,
too afraid
to descend
into the damp cave,

too weak to grasp
in my hand
the soft-winged sparrow
of my life.

Orchard Love, Fallen Deer

I am caught in the brambles.
I have seen the dead deer, I replied.
I am caught in the brambles.
I saw her throw her tampax over her right shoulder.
It is hunting season, I said.
I have always wanted you in the orchard, she said.
I do not want to rape you, she added,
climbing on top of me.
Tell me you like me a lot, sweetie.
I like you a lot, sweetie.
Tell me something original,
something I haven't said,
I want it to be an orgy,
orgy in the orchard.
We are in view of our neighbor's binoculars.
They will never see us, she said.
We will be killed just as we reach orgasm.
You keep your orange dashiki on, she said.
I love you, she said, as we lay wet together.
I love you, I said.
Let me go first on our way to the road, I added,
I do not want them to shoot you.
It would be a good movie, she said.

Lovemakings

"Pretty surreptitious," she said to me
as we put our clothes on
over still hot bodies.
I had told her
no one would notice,
at midday,
along the small creek.
It would be surreptitious,
I assured her,
as I pulled her dress up
about her waist,
burying my head deep
in her crotch.

In my studio,
sitting on my lap,
my hands search her back,
discovering her bra undone
I struggle with the buttons of her pants,
her shoes tightly laced.
We close the blinds quickly,
clothes falling about us.
She asks me later
if I love her now.
"Of course," I reply.
"How long is your refractory period?"
she asks.

Autumn afternoon
on the living room rug.
Her eyes staring down at me,
my finger probing the contours of her teeth,
sweat running down her freckled sternum,

the crystal about her neck
bumping between us.
Grabbing the clear pendant
with her right hand
she swings it
behind her back.
We are melting,
fused,
one.

Without Goodbye

I sit and look
out the backdoor screen,
thinking of John Prine
and mahamudra,
the waves of my ocean mind
simply noticing
simply seeing...
the framing of the door itself,
parallel strips of wood
forever equidistant
across the lower screen.
An equal sign
slashed
through my vision,
fir trees standing tall
straight and untouching
behind it.
Today my galaxy has changed.
A planet once riveted in space,
its distance fixed
immutable,
with silent tremor
has jarred itself free,
moved farther into orbit.
Always with unerring obedience
to its perfect laws.
A flawless orbit,
beyond the magnetism
of my heaven's history,
beyond the reach
of my galaxy's love.

Diamond Aorta

I lay in bed
next to her,
telling her
how the tears
would not come.
Telling her
the wound was deep,
how I wished
I could cry
the diamond out,
hard diamond
lodged on my heart.

If only we could
let ourselves feel
what our thick chests
protect.
Cry until
we can cry no more,
dislodge the diamond
in watery grief.
Weep until the diamond
falls before us
wet and shimmering
like a newborn
gasping for breath
as it slides
into view.

For years
that diamond bond
transfixed us,
its muted brilliance

rarely mentioned.
Our bodies
told of its presence.
Passion mixed
with silent grief,
our loving
unveiling our sorrow.
Only our eyes
spoke softly
of its deep sparkle.
Until at last
we turned
from each other,
exhausted by the fleeting glance,
the knowing look,
the inescapable mirroring
of our own pain.

East to the Birthplace of Weaving

Learn from the Sadness

Learn from the sadness
of a starless night.
Learn from the tears of a mother
near the grave of her son,
learn from the Lord Almighty
in the thundering sky
above Calvary,
learn from the Pharaoh
asleep near his first born
on a night
shattered by screams.
Learn from the swollen lips
of Africa's dark-eyed children,
learn from the families huddled silent
in Central America's countless graves,
learn from the shadows
on Nagasaki's walls,
learn from the toothless women
walking to Hitler's chambers.
Learn you shall not sacrifice
the weak.
Learn that sacrifice
in the name of freedom
leads not to the Promised Land
but to darkness.
Learn you shall not buy freedom
with another's death.

Moses,
you did not want
to serve,
living among gentle shepherds,

beholding a God
without voice,
without demands.
Until the flames
entranced you,
their righteous tongues
talking loudly
of bondage,
shouting
for freedom.
Long red tongues, licking
the barricaded front doors
of Egypt's dying children,
as God shielded his eyes
from the price
of liberation.

Moses,
was it you
on the low cross,
wood still smoldering
from that lonely pasture?
Did you hear him cry out
for his father
as the world grew still,
cry out for his father
as the world grew dark,
cry out for his father
until the pink ember heart
gave up its glow?
What is it we fear
that death
becomes our weapon,

that children must die
to hallow our myths?
Who has taught us
and whom will we teach?
Learn you shall not buy freedom
with another's death.

Taking Stock

We have been offered this:
the perfection of the perfectly tucked dive,
assuming pike position
from the 98th floor.
I avert my eyes from the screen,
horrified at the courageous resolve
of death.
Truly we have traded here...
heart for heart,
retribution for retribution,
revenge for countless revenge.
I think of family,
finding ones' way back
into family,
our individual work to be seen,
to give up the habit of anger
and war.
Were they also
demanding their way
into family?
Was there any tenderness
beneath the confusion and hatred
in their eyes?
Are we willing to look closely
into the fixed stares,
find ourselves
in those dark pools,
sense the hopelessness,
the longing,
even in those who would kill?
One act does not erase the human.
One brutal act
does not cut out the heart.

Can we connect to that heart,
can we allow ourselves
the pain and sorrow
of that connection?

Eternity

I am speaking of more
than living in the moment.
A second can stretch
into a life's eternity,
gray rubber sheet of time
pulled farther
and farther apart
until the molecules
disappear in air.
I feel the relaxation,
the sense of altered consciousness,
the pressure
inside my skull
as if the birth
of my new awareness
must push itself past
the ticking biology
of my own flesh.
My mind is a sea
of numbers and fractions,
a hot soup surging
against a fragile dam.
I am afraid of spilling
my own moment
onto the seat beside me,
bubbling and swirling
about my sweet dog's feet.
Afraid she might devour it
and then my existence
would be gone,
exactly what I walked into,
exactly how my undivided
division
began.

Prospecting

for Howard

I want to mine your sentence
my therapist said,
a transitive approach
to hidden riches.
I saw Kierkegaard
in the Sierra Madres,
face blackened
by hours of crawling
through timbered tunnels.
Kierkegaard standing
at the mine's entrance,
"either"
"ore"
he exclaimed
as the small carts
rolled past him,
"either"
"ore"
a slight smile
then the frown,
"either"
"ore"
he cried softly
as I watched him
separate the nuggets
placing them tenderly
in their black iron beds.
I could not tell
which he was seeking.
I could not tell
where his real treasure
lay.

The Soul Shows Itself

The soul shows itself
in so many ways.
Ancient mountain stream
cutting a deep canyon,
only the swirling eddies
and the rapids
bumping beneath our raft
teach us anything
of its presence.
The still fawn drinks
at water's edge
never looking up
as we race downriver.
Our delight turns quickly
to the rock wall
on river left,
her gaze never lifts
from the cool stream
near her mouth.

At night we sleep
on sandy beaches.
Each grain of sand
stolen from a dark boulder,
bleached white by the sun,
on slow journey
back to the sea.
I gaze into the soft eyes of my son,
the dark eyes of my lover,
the twinkling green eyes
of a young child.
At the very center
I find the blackness

of those boulders,
infusing our bodies
like hot lava
from deep
within the earth.

At the final bend,
as the river
winds past us,
we pull our rafts
onto the rocky shore.
We strip them
of our provisions,
lift the metal frames
off their proud blue lungs,
open the valves
to let their breath rush out.
I stand in awe
at the invisible support
of our lives.
Even the bodies
are wrapped tight,
placed on a metal trailer
destined for the highway.
I stare at the river bank,
transfixed by its emptiness,
looking for some sign
of our journey,
some permanence
beyond the river's flow.

Back at my city home,
after a restless night's sleep

on a soft bed,
I climb the concrete stairs
outside my front door,
first cup of morning coffee
cradled in my hand.
The toe of my right sandal
catches the second stair
and I tumble forward
smashing the cup
as I brace myself
in the fall.
Picking up the pieces,
I glance at the wind chime
swinging in the breeze.
My own breath comes slow, even
and a smile
breaks like a wave
across my face.

Monkdream

I had formed a trucking company
with a Buddhist monk.
His only duty was to ride shotgun
and make sure
we were never followed.
I remember the smooth baldness
of his shaved head,
the shattered glass
in the rear window
of the cab.
He had taped the glass
with silver duct tape crosses,
and he had taped one of his eyes open,
one shut.
He told me he was cutting
the cat in half.
There were animals
in the twilight of our exhaust,
long lines of animals
coughing and weaving
their way after us.
My friend claimed
he could see them,
see them clear as day,
but they were not following us.
He did not think so.

Animal Spirit

I had to remind myself
the rifle was loaded
as I stumbled
out my backdoor
in the early morning.
His large gray shape
surprised me,
such on-task wildness
walking slowly
past my bedroom window.
I thought,
carry the gun
like hunters do.
Lay it casually
across the elbow,
do not grasp
the cold metal part
leaving fingerprints
on the pristine
black chamber.
Watch your step
I told myself,
writers are killed
accidentally
trying to place
small lead pellets
in gray morning predators.
Do it for your ducks
I thought,
you are not a killer
without reason.
Writers do not kill
without reason.

My search for him
was fruitless.
He slipped past me
into my woods
so fearlessly,
until that evening,
at dinner
with my extended family,
again he appeared
to break my dream state.
He woke me
from my thoughts,
my inner dialogue,
the critic voice telling me
how my life
was incapable of change,
my choices never yeilding
their wanted results.
Red accordion heart
opens and closes,
fills with slow excitement,
until it reaches
the limits of its expansion,
too expanded for sound.
Then the collapse,
sides moving together,
until the space between the dark cloth-gills
vanishes
without sound,
too contracted
for breath.

His breathing
was slow and even.
I watched him move
along my shop wall.
At first I tried to scare him
by hissing
but he showed
no fear.
I called to my son
to bring my rifle,
my heart pounding
as I kept the weak flashlight
aimed toward him.
I fired into his face,
he turned toward my shop, then back
as I fired again.
One more shot rang out
as he fled
into the woods.

Later I thought,
how automatic,
how without thinking
I had attacked him,
as if I knew
what I was doing,
firing a gun
as I had not done
in twenty years.
Something in me
wanted him dead.

Something in me
locked into the battle,
as if at last
it was a fight
I could end
with a mere
squeeze of the trigger.

As evening fell
I could hear him
rustling in my woods,
but when I searched for him
I found no creature,
no trail of blood.
I do not know
whether he died,
whether I even wounded him,
but I remember the feeling
as I assaulted him,
the effortless motion
that carried me into action.
I remember how much
I wished for
a simple victory,
a simple death
between his eyes.

Thoughts on the Coast/Starlight

My universe
two hands,
left-handed lust
right-handed intellect,
body pallid
ruled
by desperation.
I think
and I hold back.
I think
and I act.
I think
and I regret
all action
all inaction.
I lust
and I hurt.
I deny
and I betray
my lost child.
I am searching
for my soul,
for the heart
that does not heed
thought's presence
thought's absence,
lust's drive
lust's denial.
I want to sanctify
my life.
I want to be sacred
in deeds
beyond my grasp.

Visionary

for Alan

I approached my cancer
in an analytical fashion, he said.
I thought about how molds
were used in the foundry.
Walking by bronze statues
near a church on Broadway,
I noticed places
where the bronze had run
beyond the desired shape.
The areas had been sanded,
worked smooth.
You must pack the dirt tightly
in the mold
or the bronze will run
into the vacuum.
As people grow,
the same thing happens.
There are things that are lost,
things left out,
things wanted and never gotten,
things taken.
All of these
create a vacuum.
Cancer fills these spaces
like hot bronze.

I have thought of you often
in the last twenty years, he added.
When I met new people,
I always saw
some of you in them.
I could connect to them
because of my connection

to you.
Then I would snip
that connection
and have a brand
new person.

100 Acres

Looking at it
the perfect country setup...
100 secluded acres,
a white stallion
shares lush pasture
with a three-legged cow.
After cooking dinner
the vet's wife kills herself,
needle dangling
from her arm.

So many cats
lie screaming,
avoid that one death
she once told me
as my suffering kitty
cried softly
in my arms,
avoid the death
with struggle.
We do not let them die
that way.

Susan I did not know.
Susan driving by the farm
her four-wheel drive
noisy on the gravel,
my horse's head
out the barn window
eyes full of life,
white stallion
in her veins.

Pain takes us.
Pain amidst the greenness,
pain I did not know,
frail woman
I never knew...
cold limbs
a missing leg,
a horse unbridled
gnawing in darkness
the splintered wood
of his stall.

Shree, Shree Ramana

There is a self
waiting to meet you.
No voyage of mind
will bring you closer.
No hope
that you hold to.
No action
of will or body.
Heaven and hell
are a single fire.
Bliss fades,
terror subsides,
until you find you are
in no place,
no thing.

North to Ceremony and Spirit

Path

I am seeking to become
a priest of spirit,
to hear again
the quiet song
at my core.
Not a high priest
full of magic,
not an elder
with sacred footsteps
stirring the dust
at nightfall.

I want to give up struggle
in favor of balance.
I want to comfort
those I love
with my stillness.
Not with the grandeur
of the eagle's furious ascent,
but with the fleeting beauty
of its disappearance
into the horizon.

I want to learn again
to speak the truth.
I want to learn again
to do the simple task,
to take the quiet breath,
to give the humble gift.
I want to learn again
to walk slowly,
full of awe and reverence,

open each moment
to the guiding presence
of grace.

For my Chacoan Ancestors

There is a black metal folding chair
sitting amidst the blackberries
in my lush green woods.
It sits on the ground I will hollow-out
to be my kiva,
my altar to Chaco Canyon,
home of the Anasazi,
ancient Indians
guided by spirit.

It is a wise man
who knows the sky
begins at his feet.
It is a wise man
who feels the stars
about his ankles.
It is a wise man
who finds a place
to sit
with spirit.

The Chacoans carried huge timbers
from distant dark mountains
fifty miles on foot
just to sit.
Built masonry walls
three feet thick,
studied the sun,
learned the paths
of the moon and stars,
carved straight roads
through miles of windswept desert
just to sit.

I can hear them
chanting in their kivas,
worshipping father sun
and mother earth.
I can see them sleeping
with their eyes open,
thousands of white coal fires
signaling the stars
where to shine
their brilliance.

On my black metal folding chair,
sitting amidst the blackberries
in my lush green woods,
I want to re-enter
that sacred sandstone canyon,
where earth's four directions
cross
in eternal
balance.

Wishing on a Star

I hope to meet an alien
and not be taken.
I hope to meet a space person
with skin the hues of the Grand Canyon.
I hope to meet an alien
playing in a sandbox,
pouring water over sand gardens,
being the gentle wind
for a toy boat's sail.
I hope to meet an alien
sitting next to me
in Chaco Canyon,
witnessing the power
of earth's true creators.
I hope to meet a time traveller
carrying the small book,
"Dismantling your Achievements
made Easy."
I hope to meet an alien
who whispers softly,
"We love your earth.
We will not
forsake her."

Coming Home

Salt Lake City
heat rising off the asphalt
below a third floor balcony
with a view
southwest to Chaco.
Across the shopping mall
looms the Olive Garden,
white people slow-dining
at a furious pace.
Money flows
from air-conditioned hands,
menu choices tempt
in dizzying abundance,
a leisure class
dines casually
with non-leisurely appetite.

In Bloomfield, New Mexico
at the Conoco station
in the heat of late morning,
I am struck
by the bustle,
the gas nozzles
constant in and out,
the sun-darkened workers
busy about their day.
I sense the earth's slow energy
many layers beneath their feet,
the quiet presence of a shrine
unrealized in their lives.

Perhaps wild ponies
are always prancing

in slow-motion
across the mesas.
Perhaps speeding
on the freeway
we are also just walking,
the power grids
in the distance
leading to ancient signal fires.
Perhaps we are still breathing
cool spirit
even in our frantic doing.
And my sadness
can give way
to the faith that no worlds
will be vanquished,
that stillness resides
even in this indulgence,
this blistering flight from
our own selves.

Year of the Snake / Year of the Giant Lizard

I could be compulsive
about the rock cairns
on the way to Pueblo Alto,
each stone
catching my second thought,
my second look
back down the trail,
to be sure
to be certain
I had rebuilt the marker
in a proper way.
I could be compulsive
about my knife
being with me,
about the sunblock
spread like war paint
beneath my cheekbones.
I could be compulsive
about the way I prayed,
each word
each name
each thought
each rock
stacked neatly,
marking a path
others would know
to follow.

In the late afternoon
on the trail heading east
to Wijiji,
I tell myself
I must be careful

to walk
with the sun
directly behind me,
so I can see
when I am
true
to my own
shadow.

For the Hopi

I dreamed it was the last day of niman kachina.
I dreamed it was July 16, 1945
and the priests were in their kivas.
The walls of the kivas were shaking,
feathered altars were surrounded by bright lights,
pottery danced in the air.
I saw painted racers cowering at the foot of the mesas,
sacred tablets shattering beneath dried cornstalks,
fetuses twisting in their wombs.
I saw a spruce tree thrown to the ground,
a sandstone figure with a missing right arm,
white men with binoculars.
I heard talk of destruction,
talk of useless desert and Trinity site,
talk of a missing brother,
an Anglo-Saxon mystic,
a first ritual of power.
I heard talk of ceremonies with wine and brandy,
of a small people with dark eyes,
of a sacred land without water.
I awoke on a bed of corn
with rain on my cheeks.

Face of God

I wept
uncontrolled
as my open mouth
breath
reached its full
expanse.
Shuddering
each time
my lungs filled,
trying not to think,
my face aching
as I let
myself cry
and be no more
than present
to the crying.

Afterwards I sat
in the streaming
energy.
I sat
in gratitude
and wonder.
Breathing
the soft scent
of desert sage,
breathing
the scorching sun,
breathing
the red sandstone mesas,
breathing
each atom

of blue sky,
breathing
in and out
the sweet taste
of peace.

About the author

Originally from a small town in western Pennsylvania, Anson graduated from Princeton University, then moved to New York City where he completed his novel, *Jericho*, published in 1977. His second book, *Openings*, was published in 1979 with funding from the National Endowment for the Arts. He spends most of his professional life as a jazz guitarist and jazz educator based in Portland, Oregon. His CD, *State of Grace*, was released in 1999, and he performs thoughout the Northwest and beyond. He has taught at numerous schools including New York University, Pacific University, and Portland Community College. For further information or to contact Anson, please visit ansonwright.com.